RUBÁIYÁT OF
OMAR KHAYYÁM

Rubáiyát of Omar Khayyám

Translated by
EDWARD FITZGERALD

Introduction by
LOUIS UNTERMEYER

Illustrated by
GORDON ROSS

Pocket BOOKS, INC., NEW YORK

Rubáiyát of Omar Khayyám

Pocket BOOK edition published November, 1941

1ST PRINTING: NOVEMBER, 1941

This book like all Pocket BOOKS is NOT a digest or condensation of Edward Fitz-Gerald's first and fifth versions. It is COMPLETE and unabridged.

Printed in the U. S. A.

INTRODUCTION

WHEN *he was born at Naishapur in Khorassan, some time during the latter half of the 11th century, he was called Ghiyáthuddin Abulfath Omar bin Ibráhim Al-Khayyámi. Reduced to its practical origins, the sonorous syllables indicated nothing more than that the child was the son of one Abraham, or Ibráhim, the tentmaker. The boy, familiarly known as Omar, seems to have followed his father's trade. From tent-making he graduated to science and mathematics, and in his day he was far better known as a mathematician and astronomer than as a poet. He wrote a standard work on algebra; he revised the astronomical tables; he prompted the Persian Sultan Malik-Shah to make a drastic reform of the calendar.*

During the few intervals when he was free of his computations, Omar indulged himself in the pleasures of poetry. He celebrated two intoxicants: verse and the vine. Before he died in 1123 he had composed some five hundred epigrams in quatrains, or rubais, peculiar in rhyme and pungent in effect. The stanzas were, for the most part, independent; they embodied a terse and self-contained idea. But they were connected, if not unified, by a central philosophy: a vigorous, free-thinking hedonism, a casual but frank appeal to enjoy the pleasures of life without too much reflection.

For six centuries Omar's work was unknown to the

v

western world. It remained for a secluded English country gentleman to establish the Persian poet-mathematician among the glories of literature. Edward FitzGerald was born in the village of Bredfield on March 31, 1809, into a well-to-do family. Educated at Trinity College, Cambridge, where he became a friend of Thackeray, FitzGerald did the leisurely studying and traveling which was expected of him, cultivated music and botany, and, even as a young man, was relieved when he was permitted to retire to the Suffolk countryside. There he settled himself quietly, devoted his days to his friends and his flowers, and led a pleasantly unproductive life until his late forties.

In his fiftieth year, FitzGerald published a little paper-bound pamphlet of translations which he called The Rubáiyát of Omar Khayyám. *The pamphlet was published anonymously; it attracted little attention. A year later, in 1860, the poets Swinburne and Rossetti discovered the poem. But, legend to the contrary, the work did not thereupon leap into popularity. Eight years passed before a second edition seemed advisable.*

Suddenly the poem became a favorite; the carefree quatrains of the eleventh-century Persian were used as a challenge by the nineteenth-century undergraduates, repeated by rebellious lovers, and flung out as a credo by the men and women who were growing restless if not yet insurrectionary. There had always been an undercurrent of protest against the rigid moral earnestness of the period. The Rubáiyát *served as a small but concentrated expression of the revolt against Victorian conventions, the prevailing smugness, the false acquiescence and hy-*

pocritical prudery. Religion had been confronted by science; noble ideals had come into conflict with practical necessity; roaring machinery was threatening to dispel the once pervasive "sweetness and light." The "message" of FitzGerald's Rubáiyát was something of a slogan and something of an escape; it turned imperial commercialism to an idealized paganism. Half-defiantly, half desperately the younger men and women made FitzGerald-Omar a vogue. Perhaps the most quoted quatrain of the century was:

A Book of Verses underneath the Bough
A Jug of Wine, a Loaf of Bread—and Thou
Beside me singing in the Wilderness—
Oh, Wilderness were Paradise enow!

Here was an infectious panacea, half tonic, half opiate. It was not so much a compromise of values as a combination of desirables: an avoidance of ordinary existence and a participation in a richer, if somewhat unreal, life. This was the opposite of Mrs. Grundy's middle-class taboos; this was a very denial of negations. "Wine, woman, and song" were affirmed and glorified in a mounting paean of pleasure. A Persian Ecclesiastes, through the medium of a staid English squire, assured a perplexed generation that all was vanity; that the glories of this world are better than Paradise to come; that it is wise to take the cash and let the credit go; that life is a meaningless game played by helpless pieces; that worldly ambitions turn into ashes; that in the end—an end which comes all too quickly—wine is a more trustworthy friend and a better comforter than all the philosophers.

Thrust into undesired notice by The Rubáiyát,

vii

FitzGerald attempted to live up to his reputation for a while. He published translations of the Agamemnon *and the two* Oedipus *tragedies of Sophocles; he wrote a biography of Bernard Barton, his father-in-law and friend of Charles Lamb; he made a compilation of the homely verse of George Crabbe entitled* Readings from Crabbe. *But he was not designed to be an Eminent Victorian. He was, even among retired gentlemen, unusually reticent, "an idle fellow, one whose friendship were more like loves," and his wit was kept for private communications. It was not until the letters of "Old Fitz" were published that FitzGerald's personal charm was revealed. He sank back into semi-obscurity as though it were a comfortable couch, and died, almost a quarter of a century after the publication of* The Rubáiyát, *on June 14, 1883. His end was characteristically calm. He slipped from life painlessly, almost imperceptibly.*

Appreciation of Omar-FitzGerald continued to grow. Tennyson wrote a reminiscent poem lauding the "golden Eastern lay" of "that large infidel, your Omar," and hoping that FitzGerald would welcome the verses not so much for their own sake as a tribute from

. . . one recalling gracious times,
When, in our younger London days,
You found some merit in my rhymes,
And I more pleasure in your praise.

The Persian poem which seven centuries had neglected came to life as a permanent part of English literature. Elihu Vedder emphasized, and even overstressed, its allegorical implications with his famous symbolic drawings. Translations appeared in Ger-

man, Italian, French, Danish, and Hungarian. Liza Lehmann's song cycle In a Persian Garden *was a performer's show-piece and a popular favorite at the turn of the century. Omar became a cult; commentators placed him at the head of a "literature of agnosticism." The quatrains were enthusiastically, if inconsistently, compared to the choruses in the Greek dramas, the hopeless outcries of Job, and the irresponsible drinking-songs of Anacreon. It is said that when Thomas Hardy lay dying in his eighty-eighth year, he asked to have one particular stanza read to him. It was the verse which runs:*

O Thou, who Man of baser Earth didst make,
And ev'n with Paradise devise the Snake:
    For all the Sin wherewith the Face of Man
Is blackened—Man's forgiveness give—and take!

No longer dependent upon the vagaries of a period or the tricks of fashion, The Rubáiyát *has outlived cults and commentaries. It has had its influences and imitators. Its spirit is reflected in Housman's* A Shropshire Lad, *in which fortitude and fatalism are pitted against each other and finally reconciled. Omar might well have applauded the Shropshire lad's conclusion that*

    . . . malt does more than Milton can
      To justify God's way to man—

And he would have smiled at Housman's summary in his Last Poems:

The troubles of our proud and angry dust
    Are from eternity, and shall not fail.
Bear them we can, and if we can we must.
    Shoulder the sky, my lad, and drink your ale.

But the grim philosophy scarcely matters. The cynicism may be persistent; the mood may be (as FitzGerald himself said) "a desperate sort of thing, at the bottom of all thinking men's minds." But the tune is so gay that even the pessimism seems blithe. The quick but melodic turns of the poem "tease us out of thought." We may argue about the meaning, but we are indisputably compelled and even convinced by the music.

—LOUIS UNTERMEYER

Elizabethtown
Adirondack Mountains
New York

RUBÁIYÁT OF
OMAR KHAYYÁM

Edward FitzGerald's First Version

Awake! for Morning in the Bowl of Night
Has flung the Stone that puts the Stars to Flight:
  And Lo! the Hunter of the East has caught
The Sultán's Turret in a Noose of Light.

Stone—Flinging a stone into a cup was the desert signal for
"To horse!"

II

Dreaming when Dawn's Left Hand was in the Sky
I heard a Voice within the Tavern cry,
    "Awake, my Little ones, and fill the Cup
Before Life's Liquor in its Cup be dry."

Dawn's Left Hand—False dawn, a nebulous light on the horizon about an hour before dawn.

III

And, as the Cock crew, those who stood before
The Tavern shouted—"Open then the Door.
　You know how little while we have to stay,
And, once departed, may return no more."

To The
Last Chance
Tavern
10 M.

Now the New Year reviving old Desires,
The thoughtful Soul to Solitude retires,
    Where the WHITE HAND OF MOSES on the Bough
Puts out, and Jesus from the Ground suspires.

New Year—The New Year is here conceived, as in most old calendars, as beginning at the vernal equinox (March 21). *White Hand of Moses*—In the Koran Moses draws forth his hand and it becomes magically white; and thus the bough whitens with blossoms perhaps.
Jesus—According to Persians, Jesus' breath had healing power.

V

Irám indeed is gone with all its Rose,
And Jamshýd's Sev'n-ring'd Cup where no one
knows;
But still the Vine her ancient Ruby yields,
And still a Garden by the Water blows.

Irám—A sumptuous city now buried somewhere beneath the sands of Arabia.
Jamshýd—A legendary Persian king; his was a golden divining cup whose seven rings symbolized the seven heavens, seven planets, seven seas, and which contained the elixir of life.

And David's Lips are lock't; but in divine
High piping Pélevi, with "Wine! Wine! Wine!
   Red Wine!"—the Nightingale cries to the Rose
That yellow Cheek of hers to'incarnadine.

David—He is mentioned in the Koran as a singer and is, of course, the Psalmist of the Bible; therefore, David's lips is an apt figure here.
Pélevi—An old Persian language.

Come, fill the Cup, and in the Fire of Spring
The Winter Garment of Repentance fling:
   The Bird of Time has but a little way
To fly—and Lo! The Bird is on the Wing.

VIII

And look—a thousand Blossoms with the Day
Woke—and a thousand scatter'd into Clay:
   And this first Summer Month that brings the
      Rose
Shall take Jamshýd and Kaikobád away.

Kaikobád—A semihistorical Persian warrior-king.

IX

But come with old Khayyám, and leave the Lot
Of Kaikobád and Kaikhosrú forgot:
   Let Rustum lay about him as he will,
Or Hátim Tai cry Supper—heed them not:

Kaikhosrú—A legendary Persian king.
Rustam—A legendary Persian warrior, noted for his great exploits.
Hátim Tai—A Mohammedan poet renowned for his open-handed generosity.

X

With me along some Strip of Herbage strown
That just divides the desert from the sown,
   Where name of Slave and Sultán scarce is
      known,
And pity Sultán Máhmúd on his Throne.

Máhmúd—Sultán of Ghazni (971?-1029), a Mohammedan conqueror. His realms lay in present-day Afghanistan.

Here with a Loaf of Bread beneath the Bough,
A Flask of Wine, a Book of Verse—and Thou
   Beside me singing in the Wilderness—
And Wilderness is Paradise enow.

XII

"How sweet is mortal Sovranty!"—think some:
Others—"How blest the Paradise to come!"
Ah, take the Cash in hand and waive the Rest;
Oh, the brave Music of a *distant* Drum!

Cash—Present experiences.
Rest—The future.

24

Look to the Rose that blows about us—"Lo,
Laughing," she says, "into the World I blow:
   At once the silken Tassel of my Purse
Tear, and its Treasure on the Garden throw."

Silken Tassel—The golden center of the rose.

XIV

The Worldly Hope men set their Hearts upon
Turns Ashes—or it prospers; and anon,
    Like Snow upon the Desert's dusty Face
Lighting a little Hour or two—is gone.

XV

And those who husbanded the Golden Grain,
And those who flung it to the Winds like Rain,
   Alike to no such aureate Earth are turn'd
As, buried once, Men want dug up again.

31

XVI

Think, in this batter'd Caravanserai
Whose Doorways are alternate Night and Day,
　How Sultán after Sultán with his Pomp
Abode his Hour or two, and went his way.

They say the Lion and the Lizard keep
The Courts where Jamshýd gloried and drank
      deep:
  And Bahrám, that great Hunter—the Wild Ass
Stamps o'er his Head, and he lies fast asleep.

Courts—The Throne of Jamshyd, the limestone platform of
the main palace of Persepolis.
Bahrám—A Persian. king of the Sassanian dynasty who per-
ished in a bog while pursuing his favorite quarry, a wild ass.

XVIII

I sometimes think that never blows so red
The Rose as where some buried Cæsar bled;
  That every Hyacinth the Garden wears
Dropt in its Lap from some once lovely Head.

XIX

And this delightful Herb whose tender Green
Fledges the River's Lip on which we lean—
   Ah, lean upon it lightly! for who knows
From what once lovely Lip it springs unseen!

XX

Ah! my Belovéd, fill the Cup that clears
To-day of past Regrets and future Fears—
   To-morrow?—Why, To-morrow I may be
Myself with Yesterday's Sev'n Thousand Years.

Sev'n Thousand Years—A thousand years to each of the
seven planets.

XXI

Lo! some we loved, the loveliest and the best
That Time and Fate of all their Vintage prest,
    Have drunk their Cup a Round or two before,
And one by one crept silently to Rest.

XXII

And we, that now make merry in the Room
They left, and Summer dresses in new Bloom,
    Ourselves must we beneath the Couch of Earth
Descend, ourselves to make a Couch—for whom?

XXIII

Ah, make the most of what we yet may spend,
Before we too into the Dust Descend;
    Dust into Dust, and under Dust, to lie,
Sans Wine, sans Song, sans Singer and—sans End!

Alike for those who for TO-DAY prepare,
And those that after a TO-MORROW stare,
    A Muezzín from the Tower of Darkness cries
"Fools! your Reward is neither Here nor There."

Muezzín—A Mohammedan who cries the hour of prayer.

XXV

Why, all the Saints and Sages who discuss'd
Of the Two Worlds so learnedly, are thrust
    Like foolish Prophets forth; their Words to
        Scorn
Are scatter'd, and their Mouths are stopt with
        Dust.

XXVI

Oh, come with old Khayyám, and leave the Wise
To talk; one thing is certain, that Life flies;
    One thing is certain, and the Rest is Lies;
The Flower that once has blown for ever dies.

XXVII

Myself when young did eagerly frequent
Doctor and Saint, and heard great Argument
   About it and about: but evermore
Came out by the same Door as in I went.

XXVIII

With them the Seed of Wisdom did I sow,
And with my own hand labour'd it to grow:
    And this was all the Harvest that I reap'd—
"I came like Water, and like Wind I go."

XXIX

Into this Universe, and *why* not knowing,
Nor *whence,* like Water willy-nilly flowing:
   And out of it, as Wind along the Waste,
I know not *whither,* willy-nilly blowing.

XXX

What, without asking, hither hurried *whence?*
And, without asking, *whither* hurried hence!
  Another and another Cup to drown
The Memory of this Impertinence!

XXXI

Up from Earth's Centre through the seventh Gate
I rose, and on the Throne of Saturn sate,
    And many Knots unravel'd by the Road;
But not the Knot of Human Death and Fate.

Saturn—The lord of the seventh heaven. In medieval learn-
ing the seven heavens represented the seven liberal arts;
therefore, Omar has used all the arts in attempts to solve
the riddle of the universe.

XXXII

There was a Door to which I found no Key:
There was a Veil past which I could not see:
    Some little Talk awhile of ME and THEE
There seemed—and then no more of THEE and ME.

Me and Thee—That is to say, distinct personalities as dif-
ferentiated from the depersonalized whole of existence.

XXXIII

Then to the rolling Heav'n itself I cried,
Asking, "What Lamp had Destiny to guide
   Her little Children stumbling in the Dark?"
And—"A blind understanding!" Heav'n replied.

XXXIV

Then to this earthen Bowl did I adjourn
My Lip the secret Well of Life to learn:
　　And Lip to Lip it murmur'd—"While you live,
Drink!—for once dead you never shall return."

XXXV

I think the Vessel, that with fugitive
Articulation answer'd, once did live,
    And merry-make; and the cold Lip I kiss'd
How many Kisses might it take—and give.

XXXVI

For in the Market-place, one Dusk of Day,
I watch'd the Potter thumping his wet Clay:
   And with its all obliterated Tongue
It murmur'd—"Gently, Brother, gently, pray!"

XXXVII

Ah, fill the Cup:—what boots it to repeat
How Time is slipping underneath our Feet:
    Unborn To-morrow and dead Yesterday,
Why fret about them if To-day be sweet!

The text on the armillary sphere reads: "MY SON OBSERVE THE HOUR AND FLY FROM EVIL."

XXXVIII

One Moment in Annihilation's Waste,
One Moment, of the Well of Life to taste—
    The Stars are setting, and the Caravan
Starts for the dawn of Nothing—Oh, make haste!

XXXIX

How long, how long, in infinite Pursuit
Of This and That endeavour and dispute?
  Better be merry with the fruitful Grape
Than sadden after none, or bitter, Fruit.

XL

You know, my Friends, how long since in my
     House
For a new Marriage I did make Carouse:
  Divorced old barren Reason from my Bed,
And took the Daughter of the Vine to Spouse.

XLI

For "Is" and "Is-NOT" though *with* Rule and Line,
And, "Up-and-Down *without,* I could define,
   I yet in all I only cared to know,
Was never deep in anything but—Wine.

"Is" and "Is-not"—A jest at his hairsplitting studies.

XLII

And lately, by the Tavern Door agape,
Came stealing through the Dusk an Angel Shape,
   Bearing a vessel on his Shoulder; and
He bid me taste of it; and 'twas—the Grape!

Angel Shape—Azrael, the angel of death, who watches over
the dying, and separates the soul from the body.

The Grape that can with Logic absolute
The Two-and-Seventy jarring Sects confute:
   The subtle Alchemist that in a Trice
Life's leaden Metal into Gold transmute.

Two-and-Seventy Sects—The world was said to be made up
of seventy-two religions.

The mighty Mahmúd, the victorious Lord,
That all the misbelieving and black Horde
    Of Fears and Sorrows that infest the Soul
Scatters and slays with his enchanted Sword.

Mahmúd—This alludes to the Sultán's conquest of India and its dark-skinned people.

XLV

But leave the Wise to wrangle, and with me
The Quarrel of the Universe let be:
    And, in some corner of the Hubbub coucht,
Make Game of that which makes as much of Thee.

XLVI

For in and out, above, about, below,
'Tis nothing but a Magic Shadow-show,
    Play'd in a Box whose Candle is the Sun,
Round which we Phantom Figures come and go.

Magic Shadow-show—A magic lantern composed of a cylinder, on whose inside are painted figures, which revolves around a lighted candle.

XLVII

And if the Wine you drink, the Lip you press,
End in the Nothing all Things end in—Yes—
    Then fancy while Thou art, Thou art but what
Thou shalt be—Nothing—Thou shalt not be less.

XLVIII

While the Rose blows along the River Brink,
With old Khayyám the Ruby Vintage drink:
     And when the Angel with his darker Draught
Draws up to thee—take that, and do not shrink.

XLIX

'Tis all a Chequer-board of Nights and Days
Where Destiny with Men for Pieces plays:
  Hither and thither moves, and mates, and slays,
And one by one back in the Closet lays.

Chequer-board—Used in the game of chess, which originated
in the East.

L

The Ball no Question makes of Ayes and Noes,
But Right or Left as strikes the Player goes;
   And He that toss'd Thee down into the Field,
He knows about it all—He knows—HE knows!

Ball—Used in polo, which game also originated in the East.

LI

The Moving Finger writes; and, having writ,
Moves on: nor all thy Piety nor Wit
    Shall lure it back to cancel half a Line,
Nor all thy Tears wash out a Word of it.

LII

And that inverted Bowl we call The Sky,
Whereunder crawling coop't we live and die,
  Lift not thy hands to *It* for help—for It
Rolls impotently on as Thou or I.

LIII

With Earth's first Clay They did the Last Man's
     knead,
And then of the Last Harvest sow'd the Seed:
  Yea, the first Morning of Creation wrote
What the Last Dawn of Reckoning shall read.

LIV

I tell Thee this—When, starting from the Goal,
Over the shoulders of the flaming Foal
   Of Heav'n Parwín and Mushtarí they flung,
In my predestin'd Plot of Dust and Soul.

Parwín and Mushtarí—The Pleiades and Jupiter, which were
in the ascendancy at Omar's birth.

LV

The Vine had struck a Fibre; which about
It clings my Being—let the Súfi flout;
    Of my Base Metal may be filed a Key,
That shall unlock the Door he howls without.

Súfi—A Mohammedan mystical ascetic who desires nothing
and possesses nothing.

III

LVI

And this I know: whether the one True Light,
Kindle to Love, or Wrath consume me quite,
  One Glimpse of It within the Tavern caught
Better than in the Temple lost outright.

LVII

Oh Thou who didst with Pitfall and with Gin
Beset the Road I was to wander in,
    Thou wilt not with Predestination round
Enmesh me, and impute my Fall to Sin?

Gin—A snare or trap.

LVIII

Oh Thou, who Man of baser Earth didst make,
And who with Eden didst devise the Snake;
    For all the Sin wherewith the Face of Man
Is blacken'd, Man's Forgiveness give—and take!

*   *   *   *   *

LIX

Kuza Náma

Listen again. One Evening at the Close
Of Ramazán, ere the better Moon arose,
    In that old Potter's Shop I stood alone
With the clay Population round in Rows.

Kúza Náma—"The Book of Pots."
Ramazán—The ninth month of the Mohammedan calendar, a time of strict fasting from dawn to sunset.
Better Moon—The new moon.

LX

And strange to tell, among that Earthen Lot
Some could articulate, while others not:
    And suddenly one more impatient cried—
"Who *is* the Potter, pray, and who the Pot?"

Then said another—"Surely not in vain
My substance from the common Earth was ta'en,
  That He who subtly wrought me into Shape
Should stamp me back to common Earth again."

Another said—"Why, ne'er a peevish Boy
Would break the Bowl from which he drank in
      Joy;
  Shall He that *made* the Vessel in pure Love
And Fansy, in an after Rage destroy!"

LXIII

None answer'd this; but after Silence spake
A Vessel of a more ungainly Make:
  "They sneer at me for leaning all awry;
What? did the Hand then of the Potter shake?"

LXIV

Said one—"Folks of a surly Tapster tell,
And daub his Visage with the Smoke of Hell;
   They talk of some strict Testing of us—Pish!
He's a Good Fellow, and 'twill all be well."

Surly Tapster—The devil.

LXV

Then said another with a long-drawn Sigh,
"My Clay with long oblivion is gone dry:
    But, fill me with the old familiar Juice,
Methinks I might recover by-and-bye!"

LXVI

So, while the Vessels one by one were speaking,
One spied the little Crescent all were seeking:
  And then they jogg'd each other, "Brother!
    Brother!
Hark to the Porter's Shoulder-knot a-creaking!"

        ✿   ✿   ✿   ✿   ✿

Crescent—The moon in its last quarter, nearing the end of
the month of fasting.
Porter's shoulder-knot—A shoulder pad used for carrying
heavy loads—here, for bringing up wine after the fast.

LXVII

Ah, with the Grape my fading Life provide,
And wash my Body whence the life has died,
   And in a Windingsheet of Vineleaf wrapt,
So bury me by some sweet Gardenside.

LXVIII

That ev'n my buried Ashes such a Snare
Of Perfume shall fling up into the Air,
   As not a True Believer passing by
But shall be overtaken unaware.

True Believer—That is to say, a Mohammedan.

LXIX

Indeed, the Idols I have loved so long
Have done my Credit in Men's Eye much wrong:
    Have drown'd my Honour in a shallow Cup,
And sold my Reputation for a Song.

LXX

Indeed, indeed, Repentance oft before
I swore—but was I sober when I swore?
   And then and then came Spring, and Rose-in-
      hand
My thread-bare Penitence a-pieces tore.

LXXI

And much as Wine has play'd the Infidel,
And robb'd me of my Robe of Honour—well,
    I often wonder what the Vintners buy
One half so precious as the Goods they sell.

143

LXXII

Alas, that Spring should vanish with the Rose!
That Youth's sweet-scented Manuscript should
    close!
  The Nightingale that in the Branches sang,
Ah, whence, and whither flown again, who knows!

LXXIII

Ah, Love! could thou and I with Fate conspire
To grasp this sorry Scheme of Things entire,
    Would not we shatter it to bits—and then
Re-mould it nearer to the Heart's Desire!

LXXIV

Ah, Moon of my Delight who know'st no wane,
The Moon of Heav'n is rising once again:
  How oft hereafter rising shall she look
Through this same Garden after me—in vain!

LXXV

And when Thyself with shining Foot shall pass
Among the Guests Star-scatter'd on The Grass,
   And in Thy joyous Errand reach the Spot
Where I made one—turn down an empty Glass!

TAMÁM SHUD

Tamám Shud—It is completed.

Tamam Shud

RUBÁIYÁT

OF

OMAR KHAYYÁM

THE FIFTH AND LAST EDITION

OF THE FITZGERALD TRANSLATION

I

Wake! For the Sun, who scatter'd into flight
The Stars before him from the Field of Night,
   Drives Night along with them from Heav'n, and
      strikes
The Sultán's Turret with a Shaft of Light.

II

Before the phantom of False morning died,
Methought a Voice within the Tavern cried,
   "When all the Temple is prepared within,
"Why nods the drowsy Worshiper outside?"

III

And, as the Cock crew, those who stood before
The Tavern shouted—"Open then the Door!
   "You know how little while we have to stay,
And, once departed, may return no more."

Now the New Year reviving old Desires,
The thoughtful Soul to Solitude retires,
    Where the WHITE HAND OF MOSES on the Bough
Puts out, and Jesus from the Ground suspires.

Iram indeed is gone with all his Rose,
And Jamshyd's Sev'n-ring'd Cup where no one knows;
    But still a Ruby kindles in the Vine,
And many a Garden by the Water blows.

And David's lips are lockt; but in divine
High-piping Pehleví, with "Wine! Wine! Wine!
    "Red Wine!"—the Nightingale cries to the Rose
That sallow cheek of hers to' incarnadine.

Come, fill the Cup, and in the fire of Spring
Your Winter garment of Repentance fling:
    The Bird of Time has but a little way
To flutter—and the Bird is on the Wing.

Whether at Naishápúr or Babylon,
Whether the Cup with sweet or bitter run,
    The Wine of Life keeps oozing drop by drop,
The Leaves of Life keep falling one by one.

Each Morn a thousand Roses brings, you say:
Yes, but where leaves the Rose of Yesterday?
   And this first Summer month that brings the Rose
Shall take Jamshyd and Kaikobád away.

X

Well, let it take them! What have we to do
With Kaikobád the Great, or Kaikhosrú?
   Let Zál and Rustum bluster as they will,
Or Hátim call to Supper—heed not you.

XI

With me along the strip of Herbage strown
That just divides the desert from the sown,
   Where name of Slave and Sultán is forgot—
And Peace to Mahmúd on his golden Throne!

XII

A Book of Verses underneath the Bough,
A Jug of Wine, a Loaf of Bread—and Thou
   Beside me singing in the Wilderness—
Oh, Wilderness were Paradise enow!

XIII

Some for the Glories of This World; and some
Sigh for the Prophet's Paradise to come;
   Ah, take the Cash, and let the Credit go,
Nor heed the rumble of a distant Drum!

Look to the blowing Rose about us—"Lo,
Laughing," she says, "into the world I blow,
　At once the silken tassel of my Purse
Tear, and its Treasure on the Garden throw."

And those who husbanded the Golden grain,
And those who flung it to the winds like Rain,
　Alike to no such aureate Earth are turn'd
As, buried once, Men want dug up again.

The Worldly Hope men set their Hearts upon
Turns Ashes—or it prospers; and anon,
　Like Snow upon the Desert's dusty Face,
Lighting a little hour or two—is gone.

Think, in this batter'd Caravanserai
Whose Portals are alternate Night and Day,
　How Sultán after Sultán with his Pomp
Abode his destined Hour, and went his way.

They say the Lion and the Lizard keep
The courts where Jamshyd gloried and drank deep:
　And Bahrám, the great Hunter—the Wild Ass
Stamps o'er his Head, but cannot break his Sleep.

XIX

I sometimes think that never blows so red
The Rose as where some buried Cæsar bled;
    That every Hyacinth the Garden wears
Dropt in her Lap from some once lovely Head.

XX

And this reviving Herb whose tender Green
Fledges the River-Lip on which we lean—
    Ah, lean upon it lightly! for who knows
From what once lovely Lip it springs unseen!

XXI

Ah, my Belovéd, fill the Cup that clears
To-day of past Regrets and future Fears:
    To-morrow—Why, To-morrow I may be
Myself with Yesterday's Sev'n thousand Years.

XXII

For some we loved, the loveliest and the best
That from his Vintage rolling Time hath prest,
    Have drunk their Cup a Round or two before,
And one by one crept silently to rest.

XXIII

And we, that now make merry in the Room
They left, and Summer dresses in new bloom,
    Ourselves must we beneath the Couch of Earth
Descend—ourselves to make a Couch—for whom?

Ah, make the most of what we yet may spend,
Before we too into the Dust descend;
  Dust into Dust, and under Dust to lie,
Sans Wine, sans Song, sans Singer, and—sans End!

Alike for those who for To-DAY prepare,
And those that after some To-MORROW stare,
  A Muezzín from the Tower of Darkness cries,
"Fools! your Reward is neither Here nor There."

Why, all the Saints and Sages who discuss'd
Of the Two Worlds so wisely—they are thrust
  Like foolish Prophets forth; their Words to Scorn
Are scatter'd, and their Mouths are stopt with Dust.

Myself when young did eagerly frequent
Doctor and Saint, and heard great argument
  About it and about: but evermore
Came out by the same door where in I went.

With them the seed of Wisdom did I sow,
And with mine own hand wrought to make it grow;
  And this was all the Harvest that I reap'd—
"I came like Water, and like Wind I go."

Into this Universe, and *Why* not knowing
Nor *Whence,* like Water willy-nilly flowing;
   And out of it, as Wind along the Waste,
I know not *Whither,* willy-nilly blowing.

What, without asking, hither hurried *Whence?*
And, without asking, *Whither* hurried hence!
   Oh, many a Cup of this forbidden Wine
Must drown the memory of that insolence!

Up from Earth's Center through the Seventh Gate
I rose, and on the Throne of Saturn sate,
   And many a Knot unravel'd by the Road;
But not the Master-knot of Human Fate.

There was the Door to which I found no Key;
There was the Veil through which I might not see:
   Some little talk awhile of ME and THEE
There was—and then no more of THEE and ME.

Earth could not answer; nor the Seas that mourn
In flowing Purple, of their Lord Forlorn;
   Nor rolling Heaven, with all his Signs reveal'd
And hidden by the sleeve of Night and Morn.

Then of the THEE IN ME who works behind
The Veil, I lifted up my hands to find
   A lamp amid the Darkness; and I heard,
As from Without—"THE ME WITHIN THEE BLIND!"

XXXV

Then to the Lip of this poor earthen Urn
I lean'd, the Secret of my Life to learn:
   And Lip to Lip it murmur'd—"While you live,
"Drink!—for, once dead, you never shall return."

XXXVI

I think the Vessel, that with fugitive
Articulation answer'd, once did live,
   And drink; and Ah! the passive Lip I kiss'd,
How many Kisses might it take—and give!

XXXVII

For I remember stopping by the way
To watch a Potter thumping his wet Clay:
   And with its all-obliterated Tongue
It murmur'd—"Gently, Brother, gently, pray!"

XXXVIII

And has not such a Story from of Old
Down Man's successive generations roll'd
   Of such a clod of saturated Earth
Cast by the Maker into Human mold?

And not a drop that from our Cups we throw
For Earth to drink of, but may steal below
 To quench the fire of Anguish in some Eye
There hidden—far beneath, and long ago.

As then the Tulip for her morning sup
Of Heav'nly Vintage from the soil looks up,
 Do you devoutly do the like, till Heav'n
To Earth invert you—like an empty Cup.

Perplext no more with Human or Divine,
To-morrow's tangle to the winds resign,
 And lose your fingers in the tresses of
The Cypress-slender Minister of Wine.

And if the Wine you drink, the Lip you press,
End in what All begins and ends in—Yes;
 Think then you are TO-DAY what YESTERDAY
You were—TO-MORROW you shall not be less.

So when that Angel of the darker Drink
At last shall find you by the river-brink,
 And, offering his Cup, invite your Soul
Forth to your Lips to quaff—you shall not shrink.

Why, if the Soul can fling the Dust aside,
And naked on the Air of Heaven ride,
    Were't not a Shame—were't not a Shame for him
In this clay carcass crippled to abide?

'Tis but a Tent where takes his one day's rest
A Sultán to the realm of Death addrest;
    The Sultán rises, and the dark Ferrash
Strikes, and prepares it for another Guest.

And fear not lest Existence closing your
Account, and mine, should know the like no more;
    The Eternal Sákí from that Bowl has pour'd
Millions of Bubbles like us, and will pour.

When You and I behind the Veil are past,
Oh, but the long, long while the World shall last,
    Which of our Coming and Departure heeds
As the Sea's self should heed a pebble-cast.

A Moment's Halt—a momentary taste
Of BEING from the Well amid the Waste—
    And Lo!—the phantom Caravan has reach'd
The NOTHING it set out from—Oh, make haste!

Would you that spangle of Existence spend
About THE SECRET—quick about it, Friend!
　A Hair perhaps divides the False from True—
And upon what, prithee, may life depend?

L

A Hair perhaps divides the False and True;
Yes; and a single Alif were the clue—
　Could you but find it—to the Treasure-house,
And peradventure to THE MASTER too;

LI

Whose secret Presence through Creation's veins
Running Quicksilver-like eludes your pains;
　Taking all shapes from Máh to Máhi and
They change and perish all—but He remains;

LII

A moment guessed—then back behind the Fold
Immerst of Darkness round the Drama roll'd
　Which, for the Pastime of Eternity,
He doth Himself contrive, enact, behold.

LIII

But if in vain, down on the stubborn floor
Of Earth, and up to Heav'n's unopening Door,
　You gaze TO-DAY, while You are You—how then
TO-MORROW, when You shall be You no more?

LIV

Waste not your Hour, nor in the vain pursuit
Of This and That endeavor and dispute;
   Better be jocund with the fruitful Grape
Than sadden after none, or bitter, Fruit.

LV

You know, my Friends, with what a brave Carouse
I made a Second Marriage in my house;
   Divorced old barren Reason from my Bed,
And took the Daughter of the Vine to Spouse.

LVI

For "Is" and "Is-not" though with Rule and Line
And "Up-and-down" by Logic I define,
   Of all that one should care to fathom, I
Was never deep in anything but—Wine.

LVII

Ah, by my Computations, People say,
Reduce the Year to better reckoning?—Nay,
   'Twas only striking from the Calendar
Unborn To-morrow and dead Yesterday.

LVIII

And lately, by the Tavern Door agape,
Came shining through the Dusk an Angel Shape
   Bearing a Vessel on his Shoulder; and
He bid me taste of it; and 'twas—the Grape!

The Grape that can with Logic absolute
The Two-and-Seventy jarring Sects confute:
  The sovereign Alchemist that in a trice
Life's leaden metal into Gold transmute;

The mighty Mahmúd, Allah-breathing Lord,
That all the misbelieving and black Horde
  Of Fears and Sorrows that infest the Soul
Scatters before him with his whirlwind Sword.

Why, be this Juice the growth of God, who dare
Blaspheme the twisted tendril as a Snare?
  A Blessing, we should use it, should we not?
And if a Curse—why, then, Who set it there?

I must abjure the Balm of Life, I must,
Scared by some After-reckoning ta'en on trust,
  Or lured with Hope of some Diviner Drink,
To fill the Cup—when crumbled into Dust!

Of threats of Hell and Hopes of Paradise!
One thing at least is certain—*This* Life flies;
  One thing is certain and the rest is Lies;
The Flower that once has blown for ever dies.

Strange, is it not? that of the myriads who
Before us pass'd the door of Darkness through,
    Not one returns to tell us of the Road,
Which to discover we must travel too.

The Revelations of Devout and Learn'd
Who rose before us, and as Prophets burn'd,
    Are all but Stories, which, awoke from Sleep
They told their comrades, and to Sleep return'd.

I sent my Soul through the Invisible,
Some letter of that After-life to spell:
    And by and by my Soul return'd to me,
And answer'd "I Myself am Heav'n and Hell:"

Heav'n but the Vision of fulfill'd Desire,
And Hell the Shadow from a Soul on fire,
    Cast on the Darkness into which Ourselves,
So late emerged from, shall so soon expire.

We are no other than a moving row
Of Magic Shadow-shapes that come and go
    Round with the Sun-illumined Lantern held
In Midnight by the Master of the Show;

But helpless Pieces of the Game He plays
Upon this Chequer-board of Nights and Days;
   Hither and thither moves, and checks, and slays,
And one by one back in the Closet lays.

The Ball no question makes of Ayes and Noes,
But Here or There as strikes the Player goes;
   And He that toss'd you down into the Field,
He knows about it all—HE knows—HE knows!

The Moving Finger writes; and, having writ,
Moves on: nor all your Piety nor Wit
   Shall lure it back to cancel half a Line,
Nor all your Tears wash out a Word of it.

And that inverted Bowl they call the Sky,
Whereunder crawling coop'd we live and die,
   Lift not your hands to *It* for help—for It
As impotently moves as you or I.

With Earth's first Clay They did the Last Man knead,
And there of the Last Harvest sow'd the Seed:
   And the first Morning of Creation wrote
What the Last Dawn of Reckoning shall read.

YESTERDAY *This* Day's Madness did prepare;
To-morrow's Silence, Triumph, or Despair:
    Drink! for you not know whence you came, nor
       why:
Drink! for you know not why you go nor where.

LXXV

I tell you this—When, started from the Goal,
Over the flaming shoulders of the Foal
    Of Heav'n Parwín and Mushtarí they flung,
In my predestined Plot of Dust and Soul.

LXXVI

The Vine had struck a fiber: which about
It clings my Being—let the Dervish flout;
    Of my Base metal may be filed a Key
That shall unlock the Door he howls without.

LXXVII

And this I know: whether the one True Light
Kindle to Love, or Wrath-consume me quite,
    One Flash of It within the Tavern caught
Better than in the Temple lost outright.

LXXVIII

What! out of senseless Nothing to provoke
A conscious Something to resent the yoke
    Of unpermitted Pleasure, under pain
Of Everlasting Penalties, if broke!

What! from his helpless Creature be repaid
Pure Gold for what he lent him dross-allay'd—
   Sue for a Debt he never did contract,
And cannot answer—Oh the sorry trade!

Oh Thou, who didst with pitfall and with gin
Beset the Road I was to wander in,
   Thou wilt not with Predestined Evil round
Enmesh, and then impute my Fall to Sin!

Oh Thou, who Man of baser Earth didst make,
And ev'n with Paradise devise the Snake:
   For all the Sin wherewith the Face of Man
Is blacken'd—Man's forgiveness give—and take!

    *   *   *   *   *   *

As under cover of departing Day
Slunk hunger-stricken Ramazán away,
   Once more within the Potter's house alone
I stood, surrounded by the Shapes of Clay.

Shapes of all Sorts and Sizes, great and small,
That stood along the floor and by the wall;
   And some loquacious Vessels were; and some
Listen'd perhaps, but never talk'd at all.

Said one among them—"Surely not in vain
My substance of the common Earth was ta'en
   And to this Figure molded, to be broke,
Or trampled back to shapeless Earth again."

Then said a Second—"Ne'er a peevish Boy
Would break the Bowl from which he drank in joy;
   And He that with his hand the Vessel made
Will surely not in after Wrath destroy."

After a momentary silence spake
Some Vessel of a more ungainly Make;
   "They sneer at me for leaning all awry:
What! did the Hand then of the Potter shake?"

Whereat some one of the loquacious Lot—
I think a Súfi pipkin—waxing hot—
   "All this of Pot and Potter—Tell me then,
Who is the Potter, pray, and who the Pot?"

"Why," said another, "Some there are who tell
Of one who threatens he will toss to Hell
   The luckless Pots he marr'd in making—Pish!
He's a Good Fellow, and 'twill all be well."

"Well," murmured one, "Let whoso make or buy,
My Clay with long Oblivion is gone dry:
   But fill me with the old familiar Juice,
Methinks I might recover by and by."

XC

So while the Vessels one by one were speaking,
The little Moon look'd in that all were seeking:
   And then they jogg'd each other, "Brother! Brother!
Now for the Porter's shoulders' knot a-creaking!"

❋   ❋   ❋   ❋   ❋   ❋

XCI

Ah, with the Grape my fading life provide,
And wash the Body whence the Life has died,
   And lay me, shrouded in the living Leaf,
By some not unfrequented Garden-side.

XCII

That ev'n buried Ashes such a snare
Of Vintage shall fling up into the Air
   As not a True-believer passing by
But shall be overtaken unaware.

XCIII

Indeed the Idols I have loved so long
Have done my credit in this World much wrong:
   Have drown'd my Glory in a shallow Cup,
And sold my reputation for a Song.

Indeed, indeed, Repentance oft before
I swore—but was I sober when I swore?
   And then and then came Spring, and Rose-in-hand
My thread-bare Penitence apieces tore.

And much as Wine has play'd the Infidel,
And robb'd me of my Robe of Honor—Well,
   I wonder often what the Vintners buy
One half so precious as the stuff they sell.

Yet Ah, that Spring should vanish with the Rose!
That Youth's sweet-scented manuscript should close!
   The Nightingale that in the branches sang,
Ah whence, and whither flown again, who knows!

Would but the Desert of the Fountain yield
One glimpse—if dimly, yet indeed, reveal'd,
   To which the fainting Traveler might spring,
As springs the trampled herbage of the field!

Would but some wingéd Angel ere too late
Arrest the yet unfolded Roll of Fate,
   And make the stern Recorder otherwise
Enregister, or quite obliterate!

Ah Love! could you and I with Him conspire
To grasp this sorry Scheme of Things entire,
　　Would not we shatter it to bits—and then
Re-mold it nearer to the Heart's Desire!

❊　　　❊　　　❊　　　❊　　　❊　　　❊

C

Yon rising Moon that looks for us again—
How oft hereafter will she wax and wane;
　　How oft hereafter rising look for us
Through this same Garden—and for *one* in vain!

CI

And when like her, oh Sákí, you shall pass
Among the Guests Star-scatter'd on the Grass,
　　And in your joyous errand reach the spot
Where I made One—turn down an empty Glass!

TAMAM

*Pocket*BOOKS

The greatest books, old and new, unabridged and absolutely complete, in attractive editions, at the lowest possible price—25¢ * each. Books you have always wanted to read—the time-tested favorites in fiction, biography, history, adventure, romance, inspiration and self-improvement, poems, exciting short stories, and the best mystery and detective stories.

Everything you could want in a book. Convenient to buy—at bookstores, drugstores, newsstands, chain stores and cigar stores. They fit easily in the pocket or handbag, yet they're complete, uncut, exactly as the authors wrote them—*not digests!* The type is large, clear, readable. Covers are soil-proof, waterproof, sturdy, colorful, patented PERMAGLOSS.

Ideal for reading in waiting moments; on the train; in bed; in spare time. They are also worthy of a place on the library shelf, and can form the nucleus of an enduring home library of the world's best books—at magazine prices.

WHAT FAMOUS PEOPLE SAY ABOUT *Pocket*BOOKS

LOUIS UNTERMEYER: To get a range of the world's greatest literature is difficult enough at a dollar. At 25¢, and in such an attractive format, something of a miracle.

CLIFTON FADIMAN: Your report on the uptrend of the classic, time-tested *Pocket*BOOKS shows that you and the American public are both on the right track. More power to you.

JAMES HILTON: Varying a famous epigram, one might say that never in publishing history has so much been offered to so many for so little.

SINCLAIR LEWIS: As a rival editor, I must express my envious appreciation of the titles, beauty, and unbelievable cheapness of the whole *Pocket*BOOK family.

*In the U. S. A. *Turn the page for descriptions of the books, four new titles are published each month.*

1. LOST HORIZON by *James Hilton*. Thousands who saw the haunting movie will want to read the whole story of this strange 'plane journey to Shangri-La, where Time stood still.

2. WAKE UP AND LIVE! by *Dorothea Brande*. Try this on your life, your work, your daily habits—a sound, simple success-formula that has proved it gets results!

3. FIVE GREAT TRAGEDIES OF SHAKESPEARE. His most famous, oft-quoted quintet: *King Lear, Romeo and Juliet, Macbeth, Julius Caesar, Hamlet*—complete texts, with special introduction.

4. TOPPER by *Thorne Smith*. Take a large helping of hilarious adventure, mix in generous portions of drinks, spooks, and sexes, and you have a sophisticated riot that the movie could only hint at!

7. WUTHERING HEIGHTS by *Emily Brontë*. No one who saw the powerful Academy Award movie should fail to read and own this "strangest love story ever told."

10. BAMBI by *Felix Salten*. The idyl of a forest deer. Adults will find it just as spellbinding, lingering, and utterly delightful as children will. "I hardly know of any story of animals that can stand beside this," said John Galsworthy.

11. THE GOOD EARTH by *Pearl S. Buck*. Pulitzer Prize book by Nobel Prize winner! A modern Chinese peasant, his wife, his sons, and their starkly simple, yet dramatic story, through which one sees the destiny of all men.

12. THE GREAT SHORT STORIES of de Maupassant. *A Piece of String; The Necklace; Ball-of-Fat,* and 33 others of the greatest works of this Frenchman whose genius for story-telling is unsurpassed in all literature.

17. THE CHINESE ORANGE MYSTERY by *Ellery Queen*. Your favorite sleuth staring into the dead face of a nameless nobody —and everything on the dead man had been turned backward!

19. ABRAHAM LINCOLN by *Lord Charnwood*. You will be amazed at how an Englishman recaptures the whole essence of America and a great President in this masterful 500-page volume.

20. THE RETURN OF THE NATIVE by *Thomas Hardy*. An overpowering love story in the mood of *Wuthering Heights;* laden with the passion, the tragedy, the murky atmosphere of the English heath country. A modern classic to be read and remembered.

23. THE AUTOBIOGRAPHY OF BENJAMIN FRANKLIN. Edited by Carl Van Doren, Pulitzer Prize-winning author of "Benjamin Franklin." Contains Poor Richard's Almanac, many other papers as well, revealing wit and wisdom of America's most versatile citizen. No other edition contains so much *extra* material.

28. JEEVES by *P. G. Wodehouse*. The best stories ever written by the world's funniest author, about the world's most addle-pated "young mawster" and the world's most imperturbable butler.

39. THE GREAT TALES AND POEMS OF EDGAR ALLAN POE. The Gold Bug, Pit and the Pendulum, House of Usher, Rue Morgue, and many other tales of horror and imagination; The Raven, The Bells, Lenore, Annabel Lee, other exquisite poems—!

49. MICROBE HUNTERS by *Paul de Kruif*. Twelve absorbing biographies of the world's greatest, most selfless scientists, and the endless search of each to end human suffering.

50. THE HOUSE WITHOUT A KEY by *Earl Derr Biggers*. One of the most perplexing of inimitable Charlie Chan's fascinating cases. "Seizes the reader with a grip that never relaxes."

53. THE BEST OF DAMON RUNYON. As Wodehouse is to the English, so is Runyon to the Bronxese and Brooklynese. Here are 15 stories about guys like Spanish John, Israel Ib, and Sam the Gonoph; dolls like Dream Street Rose and Lola Sapola—stories as full of lumps-in-the-throat as they are of belly-laughs!

57. AFTER SUCH PLEASURES by *Dorothy Parker*. The Waltz; From the Diary of a New York Lady; Lady with the Lamp—and nearly a dozen more, brilliant, superbly told, witty, tender, acid.

59. THINK FAST, MR. MOTO by *J. P. Marquand*. The ingratiating little Japanese detective tackles one of his most exciting cases with typical finesse, suavity, and ingenuity.

62. THE *Pocket*BOOK OF VERSE. Edited with an Introduction by *M. E. Speare, Ph.D.* A treasury of English and American favorites from every age, from Chaucer to Carl Sandburg. Nearly 250 poems by 77 of poetry's greatest figures.

63. PRIDE AND PREJUDICE by *Jane Austen*. Read the *whole* story of the delightful movie that featured Laurence Olivier and Greer Garson! Told with humor and delicate insight into the ways of men and women—a love story that will live forever.

64. WHILE THE PATIENT SLEPT by *Mignon Eberhart*. How Detective Lance O'Leary solves the most difficult problem of his amazing career in unravelling the sinister story of Federie House— "Eberhart at her best!"

65. THE FOUR MILLION by *O. Henry*. Poignant, penetrating, unforgettable stories that *are* New York. No one has yet equaled O. Henry's superb dialogue, heartbreaking surprise endings.

68. HOW TO WIN FRIENDS AND INFLUENCE PEOPLE by *Dale Carnegie*. The book which smashed all non-fiction sales rec-

ords! Bought by over 2,000,000 people! It will do for you what it has done for others—help you to discover, develop, use, and profit by your hidden assets of personality—get a better position, make more money, lead a happier married, social, and business life!

69. THE 39 STEPS by *John Buchan*. From which the suspense-laden Robert Donat movie was made—an incredible, ingenious spy-murder-mystery for the most case-hardened addict!

70. MYSTERY OF THE DEAD POLICE by *Philip MacDonald*. Ruthless, relentless murderer killing off police of London! Scotland Yard baffled! Army threatens to take over!

71. THE FRENCH POWDER MYSTERY by *Ellery Queen*. No wonder he's called the "logical successor to Sherlock Holmes" when he produces puzzlers like this one of the crumpled corpse of a beautiful woman that toppled in a store-window demonstration!

73. THE CASE OF THE VELVET CLAWS by *Erle Stanley Gardner*. Blackmail and murder threaten a much-too-beautiful woman—and Perry Mason, criminal lawyer is as busy keeping clear of the law himself as he is in saving his client!

74. THE UNPLEASANTNESS AT THE BELLONA CLUB by *Dorothy Sayers*. Another irresistible Lord Peter Wimsey mystery —for readers who keep clamoring for more Dorothy Sayers!

77. THE ROMAN HAT MYSTERY by *Ellery Queen*. "Brilliant!" "Fascinating!" "Intriguing!" were only a few of the compliments that greeted this foolproof baffler about murder in a packed theatre, blackmail, and a missing silk top-hat!

79. MURDER IN THE CALAIS COACH by *Agatha Christie*. Aboard the snowbound Orient Express, Hercule Poirot tackles a plot absolutely unique in conception and execution.

81. THE RED HOUSE MYSTERY by *A. A. Milne*. Alexander Woollcott voted this "one of the three best mystery stories of all time." Clever, unusual, stimulating, and a best-selling favorite.

82. CAPTAIN BLOOD by *Rafael Sabatini*. A two-fisted, glamour-packed thriller in the great swashbuckling tradition of Dumas! Everyone who saw either smash-hit movie version will want to read about Peter Blood, freebooter, buccaneer par excellence!

85. CLOUDS OF WITNESS by *Dorothy Sayers*. Lord Peter Wimsey comes to the defense of his own brother, on trial for murder before the House of Lords—and the murdered man his sister's fiance!

86. THE RED WIDOW MURDERS by *Carter Dickson*. The creepiest mystery setting imaginable! Who of the eight men and one woman was to draw the Ace of Spades and be escorted into the

Red Widow's Chamber—where four people had been found mysteriously dead before!

87. MISTER GLENCANNON by *Guy Gilpatric*. Cheer and lusty, hearty entertainment. More voyages to the far corners of the globe with the incomparable, incorrigible Mister Glencannon!

88. THE A.B.C. MURDERS by *Agatha Christie*. Hercule Poirot meets up with a series of murders which have only one thing in common—an ABC Railroad Guide with each corpse!

90. THE CASE OF THE SULKY GIRL by *Erle Stanley Gardner*. Fran Celane looked sulky—she was beautiful—she said she wanted to get married—and she seemed to be lying about something. That was what started one of Perry Mason's most exciting cases!

91. THE *Pocket*BOOK OF SHORT STORIES. Edited with an introduction by *M. E. Speare, Ph.D.* 440 pages of the world's great short stories by 21 outstanding masters of fiction, including Kipling, Maugham, Willa Cather, Thomas Mann, Anatole France, Chekov, Mark Twain, Hemingway, others.

92. THE *Pocket* BIBLE. A unique, personal companion for every daily occasion; printed in large, easy-to-read type. This is the famous King James Version of the Old and New Testaments, edited, abridged and specially designed for reading enjoyment.

93. GOOD-BYE, MR. CHIPS by *James Hilton*. "A tender and gentle story as warming to the heart and as nourishing to the spirit as any I can remember."—Alexander Woollcott

94. GREENMANTLE by *John Buchan*. A secret-service adventure story full of spirit, action and high heroism.

95. THE SHERLOCK HOLMES *Pocket* BOOK by *A. Conan Doyle*. Nothing is more stimulating than following Conan Doyle's famous sleuth as he unravels the most intricate of crimes.

96. BELIEVE IT OR NOT by *Robert L. Ripley*. His famous, best-selling Odyssey of incredible oddities, ransacked from every corner of the globe! Hundreds of weird, unusual, humorous facts, stories, adventures, illustrated by scores of his most entertaining cartoons—.

98. THE CIRCULAR STAIRCASE by *Mary Roberts Rinehart*. Double-death strikes at "Sunnyside"—carrying the reader along on an endless chain of thrills, laughs, breathless mystery. A masterpiece by this famous American novelist and detective writer.

99. THE ADVENTURES OF ELLERY QUEEN. If you can't get enough of your favorite book and radio detective—here are 11 *complete* Ellery Queen episodes, every one a top-notcher for chills, action, suspense!

100. THE GENERAL DIED AT DAWN by *Charles Booth*. The

complete, feverishly-paced Chinese spy mystery which was such a movie sensation with Akim Tamiroff and Gary Cooper! Never before published in America!

101. IT WALKS BY NIGHT by *John Dickson Carr*. A gruesome triple-murder; a homicidal maniac; a bride of a few hours; a Marseilles wharf-rat posing as a Russian Count; an Italian vendor of drugs—and inscrutable, Gallic-witted Inspector Bencolin—all in a three A.M. thriller!

103. The *Pocket* BOOK of GREAT DETECTIVES. Chills!!! Crimedom's greatest master sleuths—each in his most exciting and thrilling adventure. Complete. Uncut.

104. NANA by *Emile Zola*. The greatest courtesan of all time, revealed by the pen of the greatest realist in French literature.

106. THE CASE OF THE LUCKY LEGS by *Erle Stanley Gardner*. The celebrated Perry Mason, curious about a mysterious telegram and a photo of two seductive female limbs gets more deeply involved than he cares to.

107. The *Pocket* BOOK of ETIQUETTE by *Margery Wilson*. Every conceivable subject of *modern* etiquette can be gleaned from this book. It is a book of reference as well as a book to read.

108. The *Pocket* READER edited by *Philip Van Doren Stern*. Short stories, poems, articles, puzzles and a full-length novelette by famous authors including Steinbeck, Maugham, Thurber, Woollcott, Housman, Thoreau, Wodehouse and others. All complete.

109. THE SIAMESE TWIN MYSTERY by *Ellery Queen*. Trapped like animals on a lonely mountain-top house—a forest fire raging all around them—an unknown killer in a group of hysterical people—here's a Queen thriller from page one on!

110. THE *Pocket* BOOK OF BONERS. An omnibus of schoolboy howlers—"Geometry teaches us to bisex angels"—and other bits of unconscious humor. Be sure to get this book and remember—"A peek is worth two furnaces."

111. MR. PINKERTON FINDS A BODY by *David Frome*. Murder runs riot in a little street of a quiet university town. Here you'll meet the rabbitty little Mr. Pinkerton and Inspector Bull.

112. FER-DE-LANCE by *Rex Stout*. The armchair-detective, Nero Wolfe, and his indomitable henchman, Archie, again outwit the D.A. starting off with a $10,000 bet and the exhumation of the body of the college president. What they find and how they win the bet—well, read it and see!

113. ENTER A MURDERER by *Ngaio Marsh*. A murder is committed on stage as scheduled in the play, but the night a young

reporter takes the Chief Detective-Inspector of Scotland Yard to see it, it turns out to be real. Only a certain few people could have done it, and *you* know who held the gun.

114. FIVE GREAT COMEDIES by *William Shakespeare*. *As You Like It, The Merchant of Venice, The Tempest, A Midsummer Night's Dream,* and *Twelfth Night*—complete and unexpurgated, introductions by John Masefield, resumés by J. Walker McSpadden.

115. DODSWORTH by *Sinclair Lewis*. A famous author's portrait of a typical American business man. Sam Dodsworth gives up manufacturing automobiles, takes his expensive and frivolous wife abroad for an indefinite holiday and finds—disillusion and heartbreak.

116. THE CASE OF THE HOWLING DOG by *Erle Stanley Gardner*. A dog howls! A man asks Perry Mason, lawyer, if a will would stand if the maker were executed for murder! A woman is missing and then her husband is shot! The D.A. thinks he knows the answer, but when Perry Mason takes over——!

117. THE *Pocket* BOOK OF MYSTERY STORIES edited by *Lee Wright*. 18 ghostly horror tales by some of the world's most famous authors including Saki, H. G. Wells, Edgar Wallace, and Ernest Bramah. We guarantee chills and thrills galore; but be sure and lock your door and look under the bed before reading it tonight.

118. WE ARE NOT ALONE by *James Hilton*. A poignant story of a young German girl who has been befriended by the "Little Doctor" from Calderbury. His kindnesses when there was no one in the world to turn to are distorted by a jury into a clandestine love affair that sends them both to the gallows on a murder charge.

119. THE *Pocket* HISTORY OF THE WORLD by *H. G. Wells*. A complete world history by the world's most famous historian. Here you have a panoramic picture of the universe from the beginning of time right up to the present war.

120. LIFE BEGINS AT FORTY by *Walter B. Pitkin*. Gone forever are the pioneer years when the toughness and energy of youth were the only requirements of success. Here is a formula for "aged forty" that works.

121. THE ALBUM by *Mary Roberts Rinehart*. Thirteen people on The Crescent and four are murdered—by axe, gun, "accident" and the other too gruesome to mention.

122. THE SIMPLE WAY OF POISON by *Leslie Ford*. Colonel John Primrose, a new detective in *Pocket*BOOKS, helps to solve a puzzling murder in the romantic South.

123. DR. JEKYLL AND MR. HYDE and other stories, by *Robert Louis Stevenson*. A story of the complete transformation of a re-

spected doctor to a murderer. This is the picture of two sides of one man—the good and the evil. Spencer Tracy portrays this character currently in a smash-hit movie.

124. MR. PINKERTON GOES TO SCOTLAND YARD by *David Frome*. A bet that murders are committed under Scotland Yard's nose and never disclosed—a follow-up outing—leads the rabbitty little Mr. Pinkerton into the midst of one of the most famous poison cases in history. An ingenious plot! A mystery best-seller!

125. THE TRAGEDY OF X by *Ellery Queen*. "Drury Lane" solves a murder on a crowded streetcar, without leaving his Hudson river mansion. One of the best of this ever popular author.

126. THE *Pocket* DICTIONARY. Over 25,000 words; synonyms; foreign words and phrases, translated, pronounced and explained; abbreviations and forms of address; and accurate, clear up-to-date definitions—all in clear, large, readable type.

127. THE *Pocket*BOOK OF THE WAR—edited by *Quincy Howe,* news commentator on WQXR. Selections from *Let the Record Speak* by Dorothy Thompson, *Inside Europe* by John Gunther, *The Time Is Now* by Pierre Van Paassen, *Mein Kampf* by Adolf Hitler and many other best-selling books. An excellent picture of the present war, with a complete table of all important dates since 1936.

128. RUBÁIYÁT OF OMAR KHAYYAM edited by *Edward Fitz-Gerald*. 75 full page illustrations! Both the first and fifth versions. A *Pocket* BOOK special edition!

130. STRONG POISON by *Dorothy L. Sayers*. Lovely Harriet Vane is about to be convicted of murder. Lord Peter Wimsey steps in— meets her and proposes to her! How he untangles the strong web of circumstantial evidence and keeps up a running romance is too good to miss!

132. The *Pocket* QUIZ BOOK editer by *Slifer and Crittenden*. 4,000 questions and answers! Everything from Art to Aviation and Sports to Mythology. Fun for all!

133. THE BLACK CAMEL by *Earl Derr Biggers*. A beautiful motion picture star is murdered in Honolulu. A sinister fortune teller is suspected. Charlie Chan, the wily old Oriental is not to be fooled. He brings the case to a climax by having all present reenact the scene of the murder. A thriller from beginning to end!

If you cannot get certain titles you want from your dealer, order direct from Pocket BOOKS, Inc., 1230 Sixth Avenue, New York, N. Y., remitting 25 cents plus 5 cents for postage and wrapping.